Plants
and Seeds

CONTENTS

Library of Congress
Cataloging-in-Publication Data

Stidworthy, John. 1943-
Plants and seeds/John Stidworthy.
p. cm. -- (Through the microscope)
Summary: Text and microscopic
photographs introduce various forms
of plant life, their methods of
reproduction, and their assimilation of
nutrients.
ISBN 0-531-17220-1
1. Botany--Anatomy--Juvenile literature.
2. Plants--Reproduction--Juvenile
literature. 3. Photomicrography--
Juvenile literature. [1. Botany.] I. Title. II.
Series.
QK671.S835 1990
581--dc20   89-26047 CIP AC

Design David West
Children's Book Design
Author John Stidworthy
Editor Roger Vlitos
Researcher C. Weston-Baker
Illustrated by Ron Hayward

*First published in
the United States in 1990 by*
Gloucester Press
387 Park Avenue South
New York NY 10016

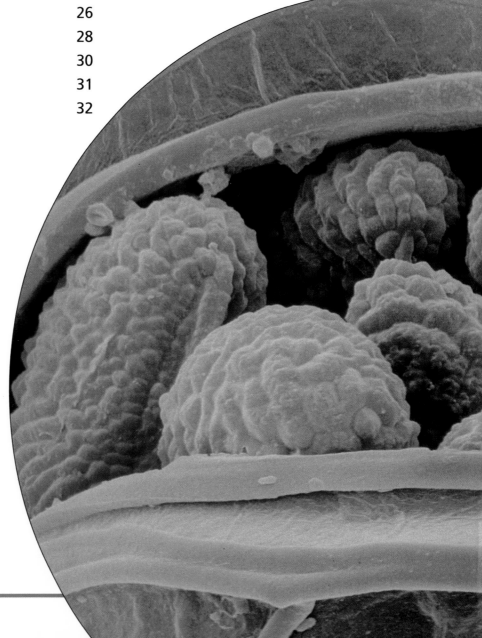

THROUGH · THE · MICROSCOPE

Plants and Seeds

John Stidworthy

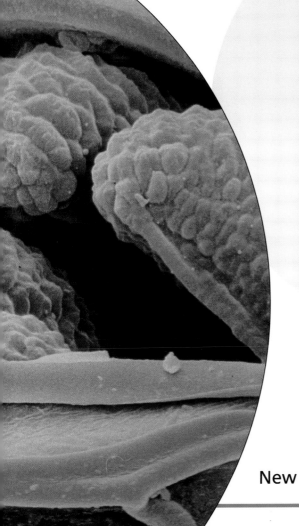

GLOUCESTER PRESS
New York : London : Toronto: Sydney

LOOKING CLOSER

Microscopes and magnifying glasses work by using lenses and light. A lens is usually a thin, circular glass, thicker in the middle, which bends rays of light so that when you look through it an object appears enlarged. A microscope uses several lenses. It will also have a set of adjustments to give you a choice over how much you want to magnify.

When we want to view something under a microscope, it must be small enough to fit on a glass slide. This is put on the stage over the mirror and light is reflected through so that the lenses inside can magnify the view for us. But not all microscopes work this way. The greatest detail can be seen with an electron microscope which uses electron beams and electromagnets.

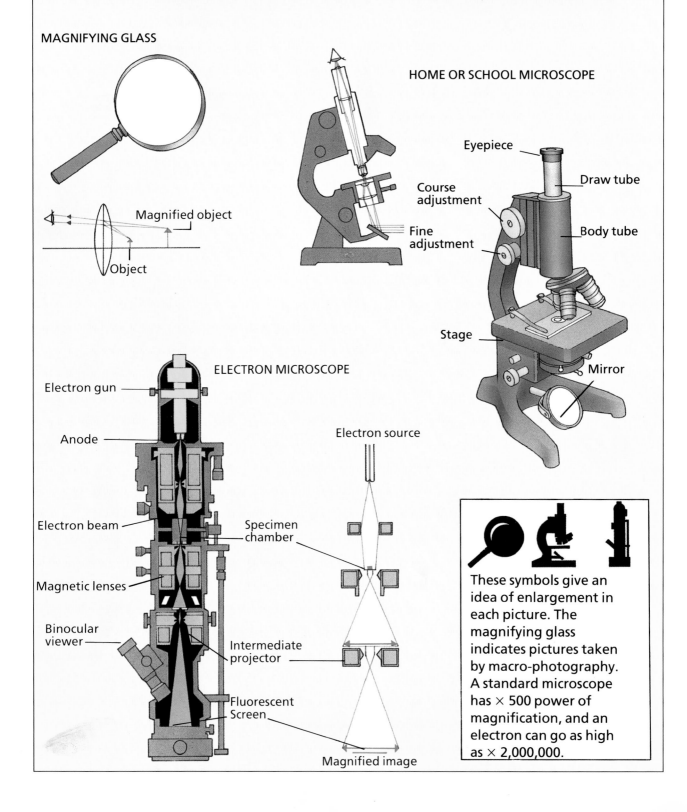

MAGNIFYING GLASS

Magnified object

Object

HOME OR SCHOOL MICROSCOPE

Eyepiece

Draw tube

Course adjustment

Fine adjustment

Body tube

Stage

Mirror

ELECTRON MICROSCOPE

Electron gun

Anode

Electron beam

Magnetic lenses

Binocular viewer

Specimen chamber

Intermediate projector

Fluorescent Screen

Electron source

Magnified image

These symbols give an idea of enlargement in each picture. The magnifying glass indicates pictures taken by macro-photography. A standard microscope has × 500 power of magnification, and an electron can go as high as × 2,000,000.

INTRODUCTION

This book contains photos of plants taken through microscopes or with close-up lenses on cameras. Next to each picture is a symbol showing how each was made. This will give you an idea of the number of times (written ×) each has been magnified compared with actual size.

Drawings appear alongside to help explain what the microscopes show. Like us, plants are made of large numbers of tiny building units called cells. In this book we look in turn at various kinds of plants, and the cells inside them, as shown below. You can see their beauty and complexity.

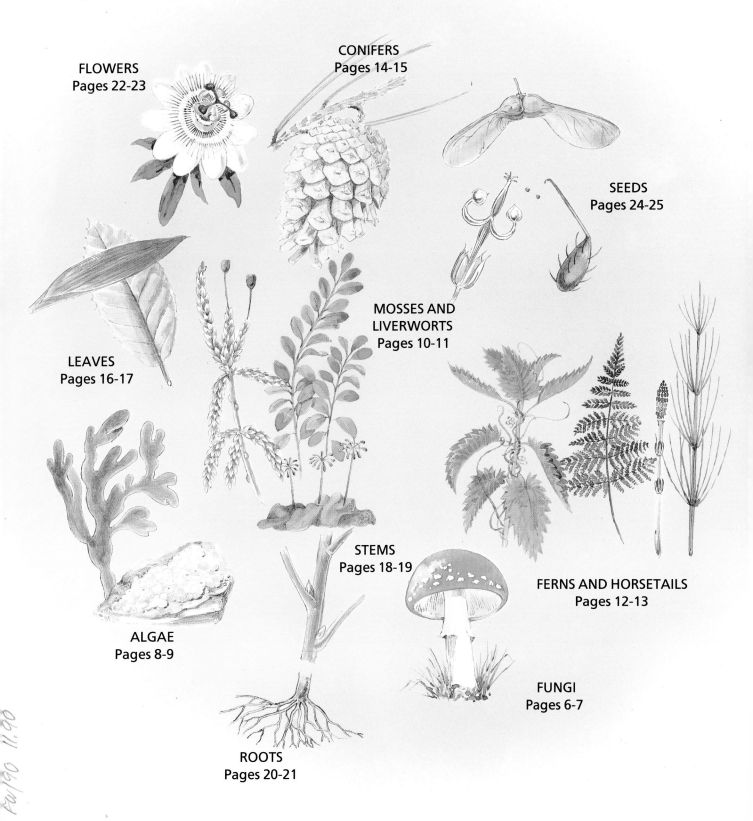

FLOWERS
Pages 22-23

CONIFERS
Pages 14-15

SEEDS
Pages 24-25

LEAVES
Pages 16-17

MOSSES AND
LIVERWORTS
Pages 10-11

ALGAE
Pages 8-9

STEMS
Pages 18-19

FERNS AND HORSETAILS
Pages 12-13

FUNGI
Pages 6-7

ROOTS
Pages 20-21

FUNGI

Unlike true plants, fungi have no green chlorophyll, and cannot trap sunlight to help make food. Instead, many live as parasites on green plants or on animals. Others feed on dead or decaying plant and animal bodies. Yeasts are fungi that consist of just one cell. Most fungi, though, are made up of a mass of branching threads spreading over, or through, their food. These threads have a wall made of chitin, a tough material like that of insect skins. Every so often the fungus sends up a "fruiting body" which contains spores. Spores are released into the air and settle to grow into new fungi. Fruiting bodies may be simple, like the 'pin-heads' on bread mold, or they may be large like the toadstools and mushrooms.

In the photo (right) you can see a mold growing on a lemon. It has spread over the surface of the overripe fruit taking nourishment from it. This is at x14 magnification. The scanning electron microscope photo (far right) of bread mold was taken at x55 magnification. You can clearly see the network of threads, called *hyphae*, of this fungus as it spreads over and into a piece of bread. The deeper hyphae are very thin. Coming up from the mass of hyphae are stout vertical ones. Each is topped by a round fruiting body called a *sporangium*. It bursts when ripe to release the spores within.

Sporangium

Spores

Network of hyphae

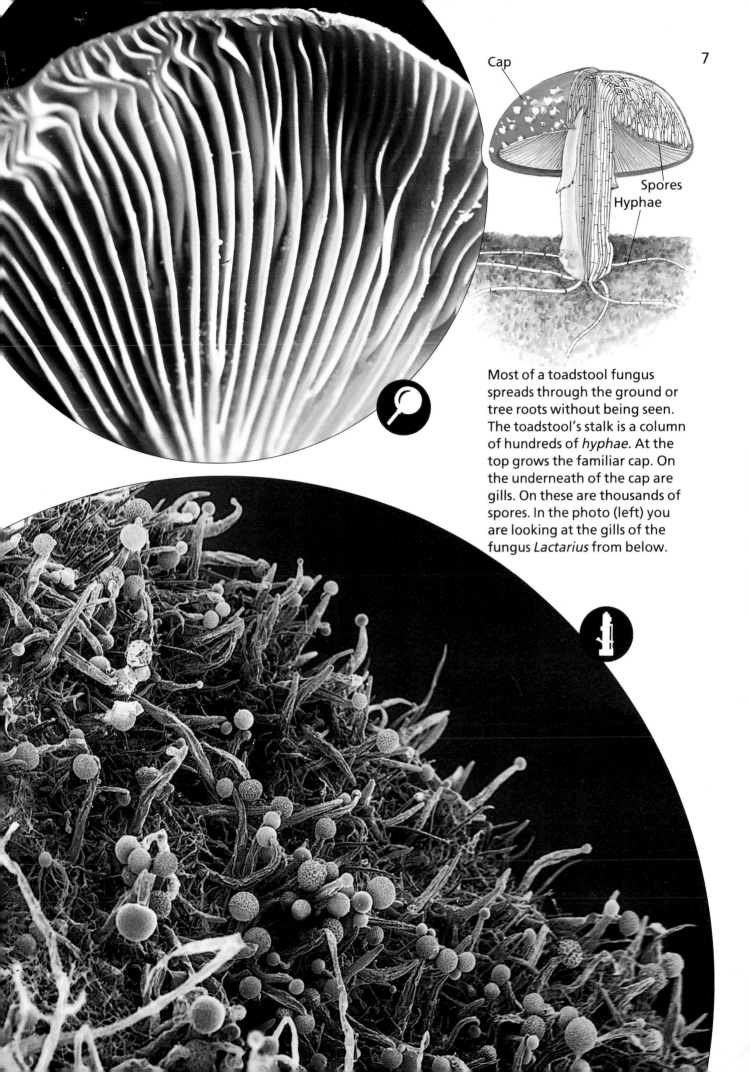

Cap

Spores

Hyphae

Most of a toadstool fungus spreads through the ground or tree roots without being seen. The toadstool's stalk is a column of hundreds of *hyphae*. At the top grows the familiar cap. On the underneath of the cap are gills. On these are thousands of spores. In the photo (left) you are looking at the gills of the fungus *Lactarius* from below.

ALGAE

Algae are simple plants which have chlorophyll and make their own food, but have no true roots, stems or leaves. The largest of the algae are the big seaweeds, but many kinds of algae are tiny. They live in sea water, freshwater, and in damp places. Some are single-celled, and can only be seen under the microscope, although there may be so many of them that they color the water or make a tree trunk's surface green. Others, such as *Spirogyra*, consist of a long chain of similar cells. Such chains may form a green scum on fresh water. Some algae live with fungi, the two combining to form the type of plant known as a lichen. The fungus provides shelter for the algae. Algae make food that the fungus can use.

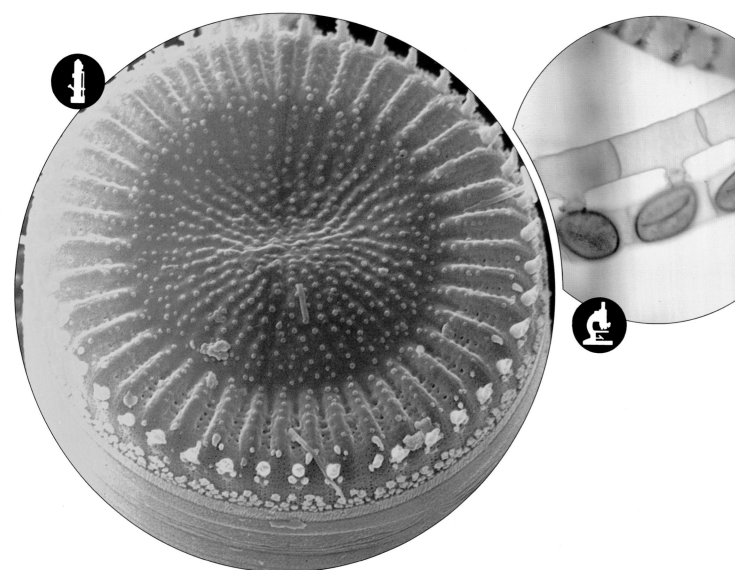

Cyclotella (photo above) is a diatom. Diatoms are single-celled algae that have a glassy shell in two parts. You can see here an electron microscope image of the "sculptured" upper shell of this lake-living alga, 0.002 inches across in life-size.

Spirogyra is an alga with cells joined end to end in a long thread as thick as a human hair. Above you can see two threads whose cells are taking part in a type of "mating." The cell contents of one thread have moved to join cells in the other.

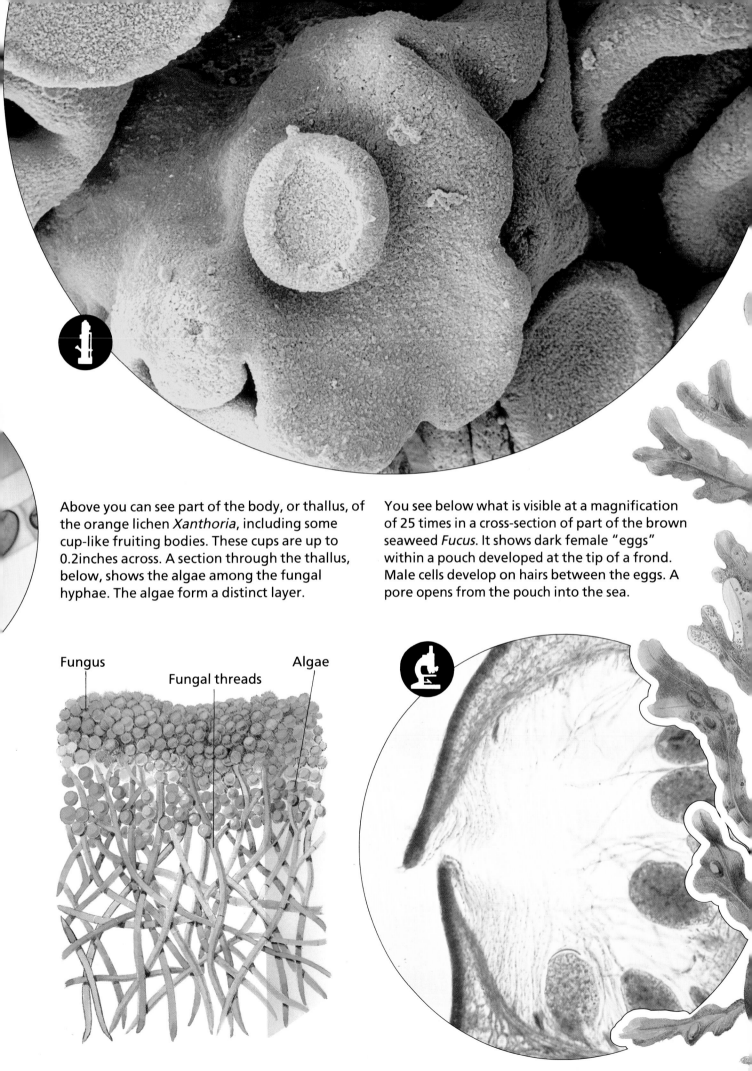

Above you can see part of the body, or thallus, of the orange lichen *Xanthoria*, including some cup-like fruiting bodies. These cups are up to 0.2inches across. A section through the thallus, below, shows the algae among the fungal hyphae. The algae form a distinct layer.

You see below what is visible at a magnification of 25 times in a cross-section of part of the brown seaweed *Fucus*. It shows dark female "eggs" within a pouch developed at the tip of a frond. Male cells develop on hairs between the eggs. A pore opens from the pouch into the sea.

Fungus

Fungal threads

Algae

MOSSES AND LIVERWORTS

Mosses and liverworts are simple land plants that flourish in damp and shady places. Liverworts usually have a flat green body, or thallus, which may be divided into lobes. Simple hair-like roots grow below it. Sometimes you can see spore capsules growing upward on stalks. Liverworts also reproduce using gemmae, small pieces of adult tissue that can develop into complete new plants. Moss plants look more complex than liverworts. They have a stem with flat leaves branching from it. These leaves are mostly just one cell thick. The stem cells look rather similar to one another, but cells in the center carry water up, and around these are cells that carry food substances. Spore capsules may be seen, often on the end of long stalks.

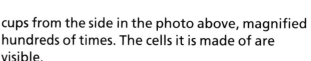

The liverwort *Marchantia* grows on marshes, and in greenhouses. Its spreading thallus (shown above left) often bears little cups holding disk-shaped gemmae. You can see one of these cups from the side in the photo above, magnified hundreds of times. The cells it is made of are visible.

Mosses and liverworts have male and female structures on the thallus. In the photo below you can see the female parts at the tip of a *Funaria* moss, as you would through a microscope magnifying 30 times. The stout columns are the female parts, and have egg cells lower down. Sperms swim from the male part of the plant across its damp surface to fertilize the eggs in the female part. An egg then develops into a new plant, the sporophyte. This stays attached to its parent.

Spore Capsule

Lid

The sporophyte becomes a stalk with a spore capsule on the end. You can see (photo above-right) capsules growing on a moss. These have a lid which breaks off (see illustration) when the spores are ripe, leaving, in *Funaria*, a double ring of "teeth" (photo-right). In dry conditions, these teeth allow the spores to escape.

FERNS AND HORSETAILS

Ferns and horsetails are the most "primitive" plants to have a special system of tubes within them to carry water and food through the plant. However, they have no flowers. In fact, the ferns that you see spreading their fronds are spore-bearing plants, more or less equivalent to the stalk and spore capsule of a liverwort or moss (see pages 10-11). The stage in the fern's life history when it has sex cells is as a relatively tiny flat plant, like a liverwort, and called a *prothallus*. For sexual reproduction to take place it needs damp conditions, so ferns are most common in damp places. On these pages you can see close-ups of some of the parts that ferns and horsetails use in their reproduction.

— Green branches

Leaves

Spore capsule

Horsetail cone

Horsetails have shoots, with small scaly leaves pressed to them. Rings of thin branches grow at intervals up the shoot. At the tip of some shoots grow the "cones." These may be a few inches long. Each is a cluster of rounded spore capsules which are attached to the shoot by short stalks. (See illustration left).

In the photo above you can see the cone of the Common horsetail Equisetum arvense. This has its cones on special shoots which are pink-brown, and does not have rings of green branches. The spores ripen and are shed in early summer leaving the green branched ones. Then the cone-bearing shoots die.

Spore capsule (Sporangium)

Spores

Sorus

If you look under a mature fern frond you often find rows of brown patches. These are called sori, and are clusters of spore capsules (called sporangia). Each sporangium has a ring of special cells around its rim. As these dry out, they first split the sporangium into two, exposing the spores, then snap back, flinging ripe spores out. In the photo above you can see sporangia of the Polypody fern. In the middle, one has burst and you can see the spores. A spore that lands and survives grows into a prothallus about 0.4 inches long. Male and female cells develop in special pouches on its underside. Male cells swim to fertilize female cells on another prothallus. The new embryo plant grows out from the prothallus. (Photo left).

CONIFERS

Some of the largest trees on earth are conifers. Conifers have needle-leaves, and are tough enough to live in many cold places. They have roots and stems with complicated systems of tubes for getting water and food through the plant. They have true seeds, and these develop in the cones on the tree. Conifers have both male and female cones. The small male cones produce large numbers of pollen grains which are carried by the wind to the larger female cones, where some come to rest over the ovules containing the female "eggs." In the pine it can take nearly a year for the pollen to grow down to fertilize the egg. After this, it takes two years for the seed to ripen, and for the woody female cone to open to release it.

Below-right you can see a photograph of a thin slice from the middle of a pine cone. The scales stretch from the core of the cone to the outside. Nestling at the base of some you can see the ovules with eggs inside. After fertilization, food reserves are added around the embryo, then a tough winged coat. The seed is then complete.

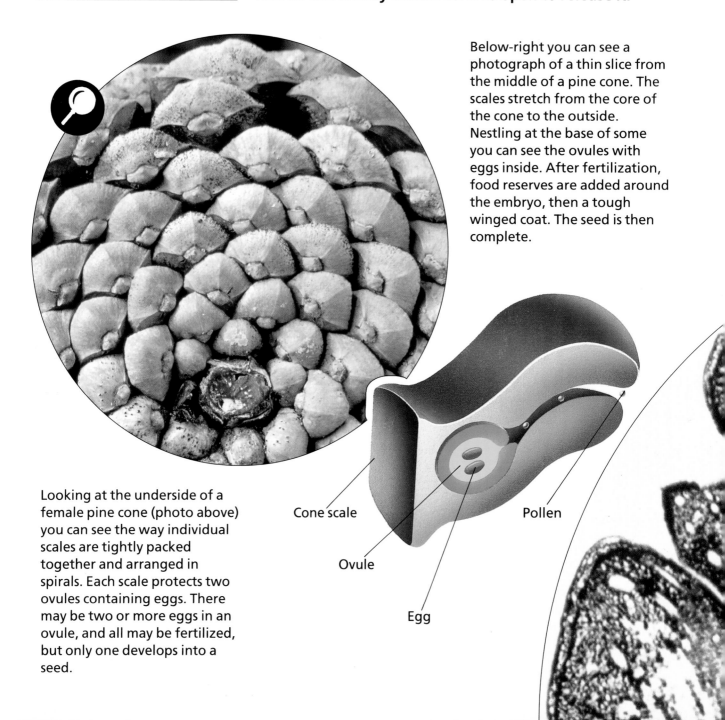

Cone scale

Ovule

Egg

Pollen

Looking at the underside of a female pine cone (photo above) you can see the way individual scales are tightly packed together and arranged in spirals. Each scale protects two ovules containing eggs. There may be two or more eggs in an ovule, and all may be fertilized, but only one develops into a seed.

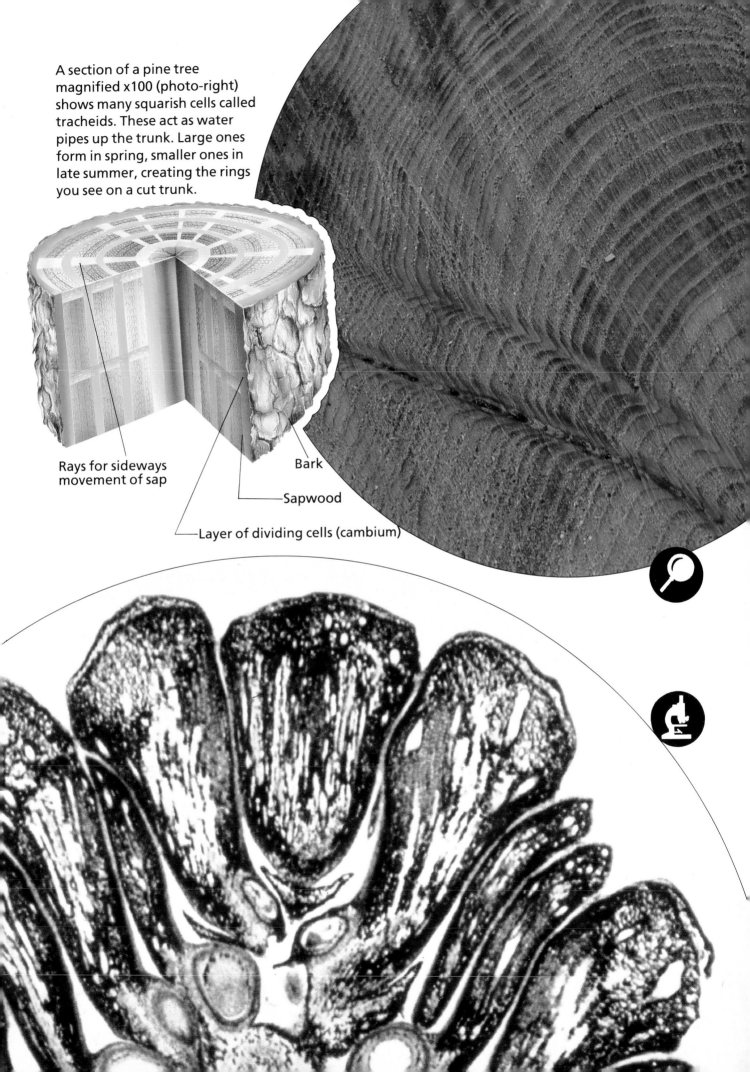

A section of a pine tree magnified x100 (photo-right) shows many squarish cells called tracheids. These act as water pipes up the trunk. Large ones form in spring, smaller ones in late summer, creating the rings you see on a cut trunk.

Rays for sideways movement of sap

Bark

Sapwood

Layer of dividing cells (cambium)

FLOWERING PLANT LEAVES

The leaf of a flowering plant is busy producing food for the plant. It is green because it contains chlorophyll that traps light for the plant to use. Some leaves, such as those of copper beech, have other colors but the all-important chlorophyll is still there. Most leaves are flat, and have a wide surface exposed to sunlight. Into the leaf run pipes made of cells that bring water carried up from the roots of the plant. Others may carry foods and salts in solution. As well as light and water, plants need carbon dioxide gas to make food. Under the leaf are many pores, called stomata, through which the plant can take in or let out gases. The leaf surface may have other structures, including "hairs" of various kinds.

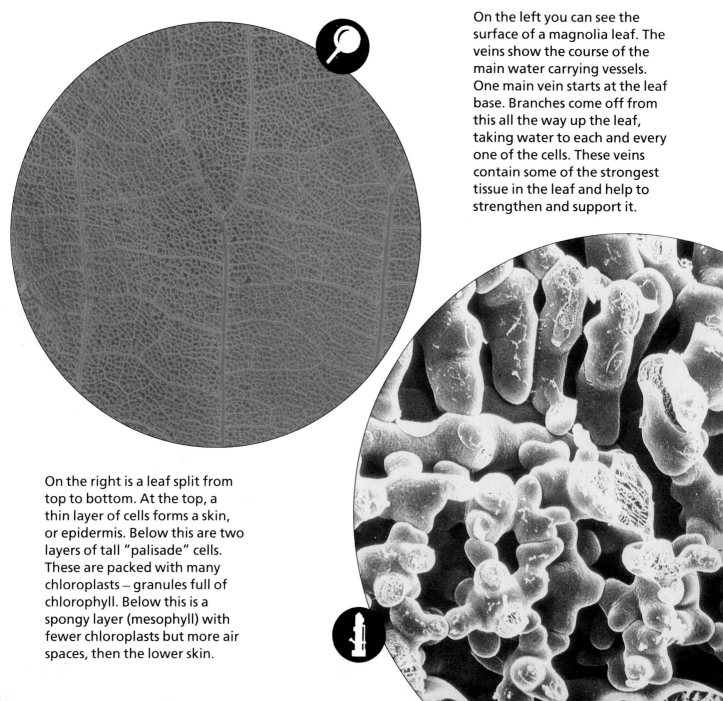

On the left you can see the surface of a magnolia leaf. The veins show the course of the main water carrying vessels. One main vein starts at the leaf base. Branches come off from this all the way up the leaf, taking water to each and every one of the cells. These veins contain some of the strongest tissue in the leaf and help to strengthen and support it.

On the right is a leaf split from top to bottom. At the top, a thin layer of cells forms a skin, or epidermis. Below this are two layers of tall "palisade" cells. These are packed with many chloroplasts – granules full of chlorophyll. Below this is a spongy layer (mesophyll) with fewer chloroplasts but more air spaces, then the lower skin.

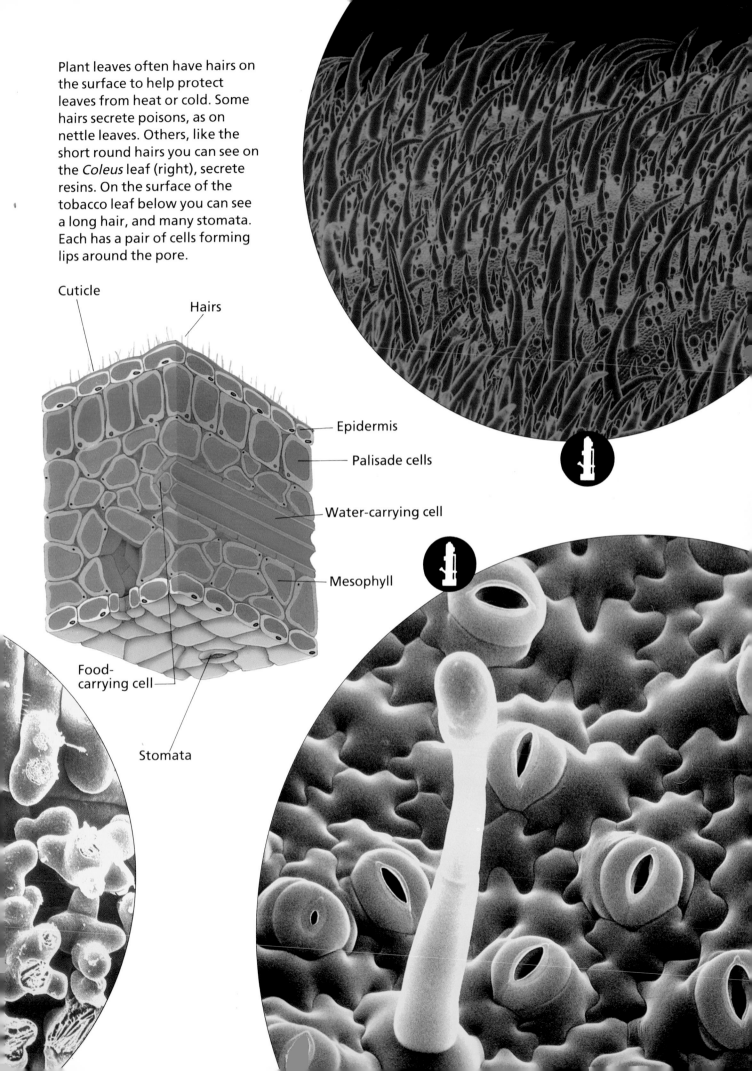

Plant leaves often have hairs on the surface to help protect leaves from heat or cold. Some hairs secrete poisons, as on nettle leaves. Others, like the short round hairs you can see on the *Coleus* leaf (right), secrete resins. On the surface of the tobacco leaf below you can see a long hair, and many stomata. Each has a pair of cells forming lips around the pore.

Cuticle

Hairs

Epidermis

Palisade cells

Water-carrying cell

Mesophyll

Food-carrying cell

Stomata

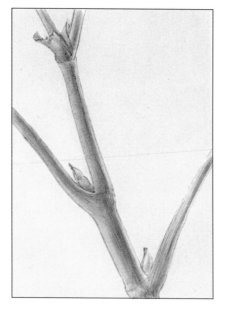

STEMS

Stems of most plants grow upwards toward the light. They carry leaves, and may branch, or they may have buds where new shoots will develop. There may be stomata on their surfaces, and some grow hairs or even spines. It is the job of a stem to hold leaves up toward the light so they can make the best use of it, and to keep the leaves supplied with water and minerals so they can do their job. "Pipes" carrying water and food run up the stem, and branch into the leaves. The pipes are made of specialized cells produced as the plant grows. Some of these cells are toughened with thick cell walls. They form bundles of pipes near the outside of the stem. Here they can also stop the stem from being bent by wind and weather.

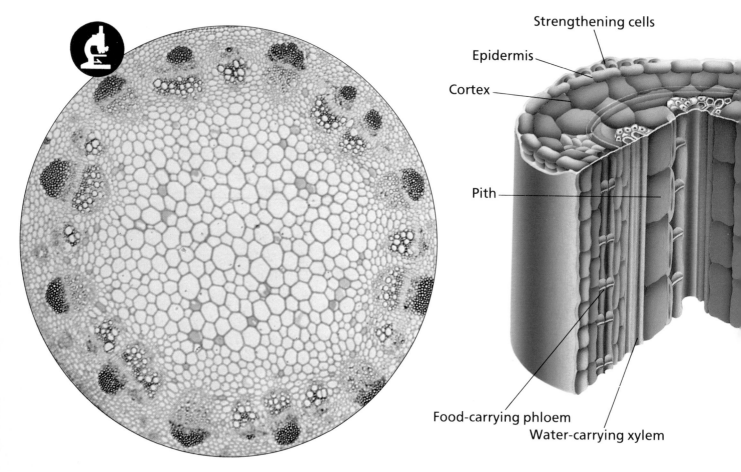

Strengthening cells
Epidermis
Cortex
Pith
Food-carrying phloem
Water-carrying xylem

Above you can see a cut through the young stem of a sunflower plant. In the middle the pith cells are fairly large and open, but around the outside of the stem you can see the bundles of more tightly-packed cells that form the plant's pipework. Each bundle has cells called xylem in a bunch towards the pith. These are the water-conducting cells. Nearer the surface are phloem cells that carry foods. Outside these there are some tight-packed strengthening fibers, cells with thick cell walls and small centers. There are more strengthening cells just below the skin.

Between the phloem and the xylem is a thin band of cells called the cambium. These are dividing cells that produce new xylem and phloem. A thin band of cambium goes around the stem between the pipe and bundles. In older stems it produces xylem and phloem all around the stem, so you cannot see bundles of pipes, but get a stem with a woody cross-section.

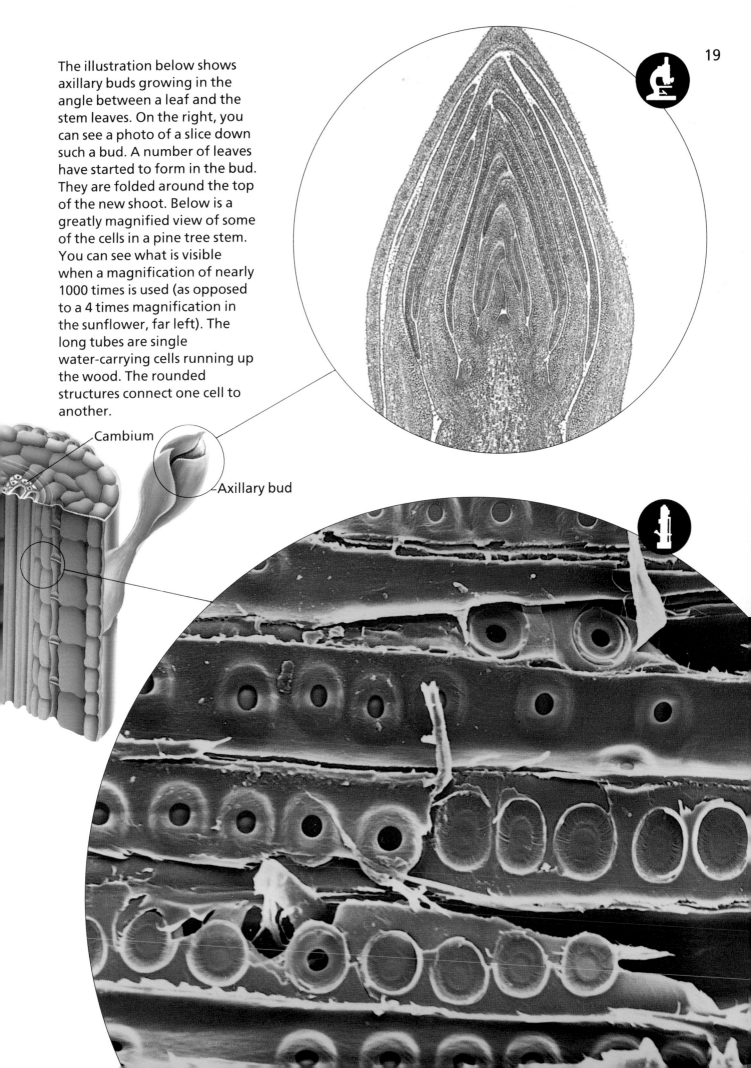

The illustration below shows axillary buds growing in the angle between a leaf and the stem leaves. On the right, you can see a photo of a slice down such a bud. A number of leaves have started to form in the bud. They are folded around the top of the new shoot. Below is a greatly magnified view of some of the cells in a pine tree stem. You can see what is visible when a magnification of nearly 1000 times is used (as opposed to a 4 times magnification in the sunflower, far left). The long tubes are single water-carrying cells running up the wood. The rounded structures connect one cell to another.

Cambium

Axillary bud

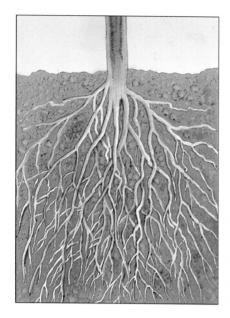

ROOTS

Roots anchor the plant in the soil and take up water from the soil so that the plant can live and grow. Water is taken in through fine root hairs that stick out into the surrounding earth. These hairs are extensions of the cells of the epidermis. Water moves through the root tissue into the xylem, and flows up to the stem. The pipework of a root runs up through the middle. In the roots of some plants, especially those of the pea family, certain bacteria live. These can take nitrogen from the air and turn it into a form the plant can use for growth. The bacteria multiply, surrounded by root tissue, forming little nodules like this one, one hundredth of an inch across which you can see (photo right) on the surface of a pea root.

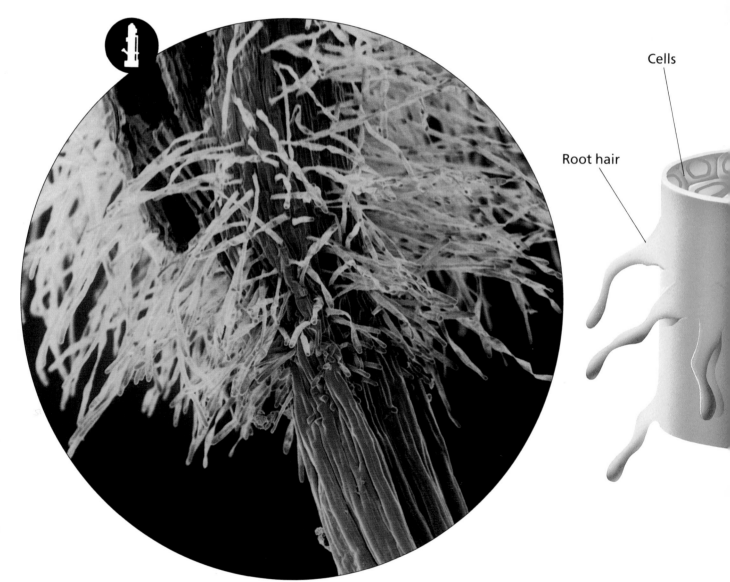

Cells

Root hair

When a root is magnified 100 times, you can easily see the tangle of root hairs covering the surface almost down to its tip. Most plants can take up all the water they need using just a small proportion of these hairs, but as water may not be evenly distributed in the soil, it pays to have a good network. Root hairs are short-lived, but new ones keep being produced near the tip.

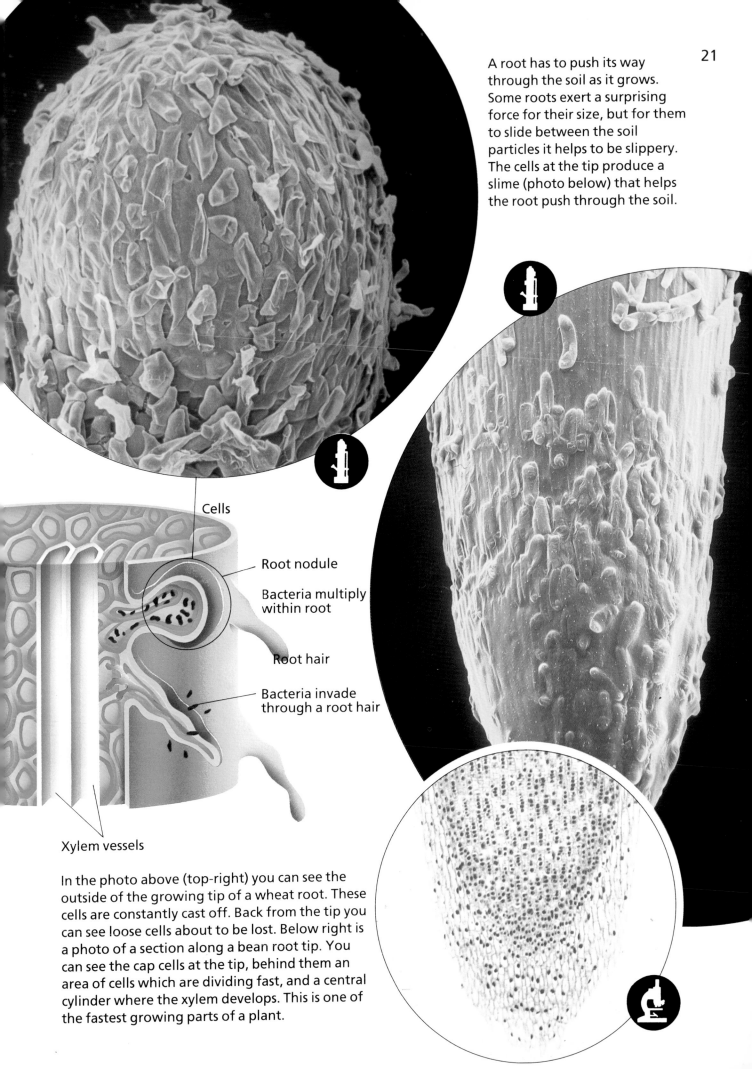

A root has to push its way through the soil as it grows. Some roots exert a surprising force for their size, but for them to slide between the soil particles it helps to be slippery. The cells at the tip produce a slime (photo below) that helps the root push through the soil.

Cells

Root nodule

Bacteria multiply within root

Root hair

Bacteria invade through a root hair

Xylem vessels

In the photo above (top-right) you can see the outside of the growing tip of a wheat root. These cells are constantly cast off. Back from the tip you can see loose cells about to be lost. Below right is a photo of a section along a bean root tip. You can see the cap cells at the tip, behind them an area of cells which are dividing fast, and a central cylinder where the xylem develops. This is one of the fastest growing parts of a plant.

FLOWERS

Flowers are devices to make sure that the plant reproduces successfully. Many of them are pretty, with bright petals or other colored parts. They often smell fragrant. However, their attractiveness is not really directed at humans, but at insects that can help carry pollen between flowers. Others may have their pollen carried by the wind. The pollen of a flower grows on the stamen, the male part of the plant. The egg, or ovule, is tucked away inside the ovary within the female part of the flower. Above the ovary is the stigma, the surface on which the pollen must land to reach the ovary. In some flowers the stigma is on a stalk, called the style. The stigma may have glands or hairs to help hold the pollen.

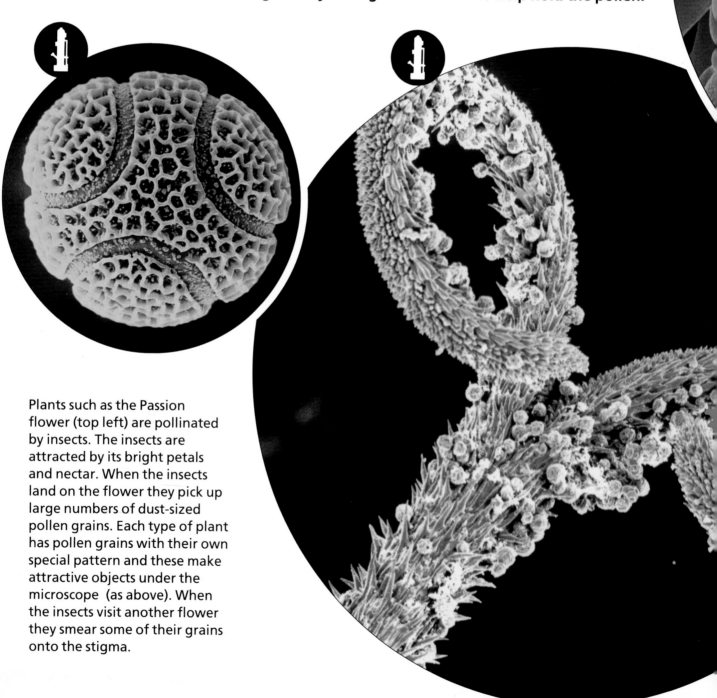

Plants such as the Passion flower (top left) are pollinated by insects. The insects are attracted by its bright petals and nectar. When the insects land on the flower they pick up large numbers of dust-sized pollen grains. Each type of plant has pollen grains with their own special pattern and these make attractive objects under the microscope (as above). When the insects visit another flower they smear some of their grains onto the stigma.

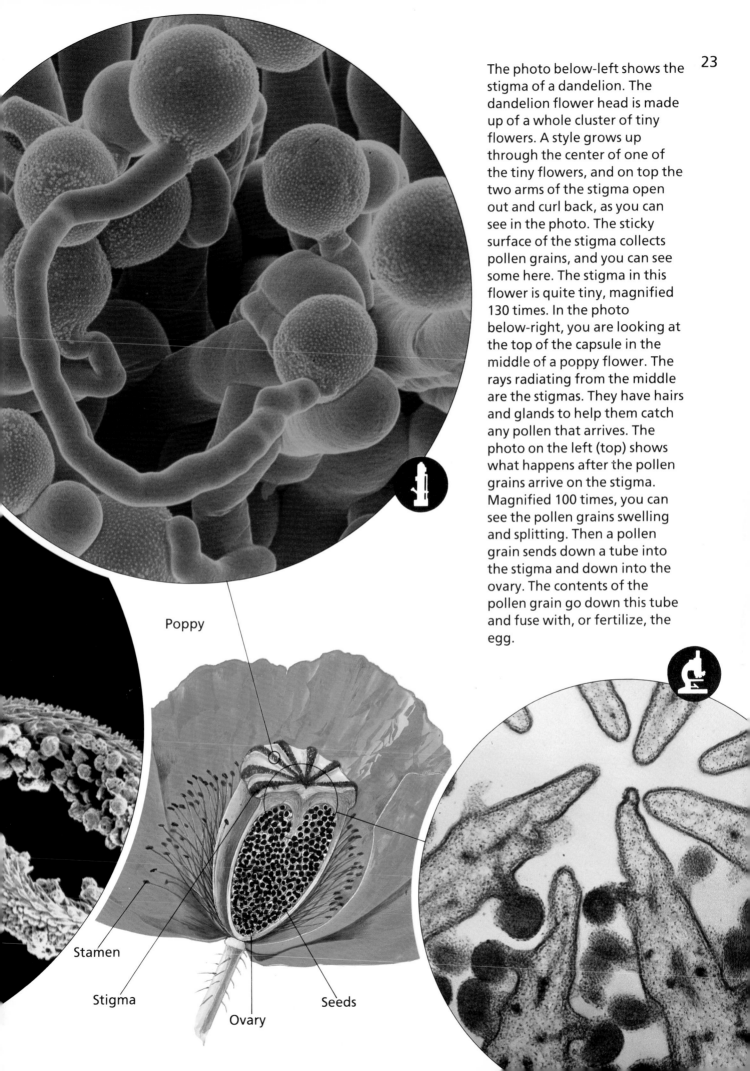

The photo below-left shows the stigma of a dandelion. The dandelion flower head is made up of a whole cluster of tiny flowers. A style grows up through the center of one of the tiny flowers, and on top the two arms of the stigma open out and curl back, as you can see in the photo. The sticky surface of the stigma collects pollen grains, and you can see some here. The stigma in this flower is quite tiny, magnified 130 times. In the photo below-right, you are looking at the top of the capsule in the middle of a poppy flower. The rays radiating from the middle are the stigmas. They have hairs and glands to help them catch any pollen that arrives. The photo on the left (top) shows what happens after the pollen grains arrive on the stigma. Magnified 100 times, you can see the pollen grains swelling and splitting. Then a pollen grain sends down a tube into the stigma and down into the ovary. The contents of the pollen grain go down this tube and fuse with, or fertilize, the egg.

Poppy

Stamen

Stigma

Ovary

Seeds

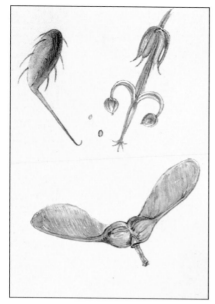

SEEDS

A seed contains the embryo of a new plant, and also food for the first stages of its growth. In a tiny seed the food supply is small, but in a bean or nut the food reserves are very large. Within a seed it is usually possible to recognize the beginnings of the root (the radicle) and the stem (the plumule). There are also seed-leaves, called cotyledons. There are two in most kinds of flowering plant, but just one in grasses and related narrow-leaved plants. The cotyledons are special storage leaves, and their fleshy bulk contains food that may take up most of the seed. Often seeds form part of a fruit, the structure that develops from a ripe ovary. Some fruits, such as an acorn, have a single seed. Others, like tomatoes, have dozens.

The okra, or lady's finger, has a narrow edible fruit about 4 inches long. In the cross section (photo left) you can see seeds arranged around a central core, with a fleshy wall outside. The stored food in the seeds contains a high proportion of oil.

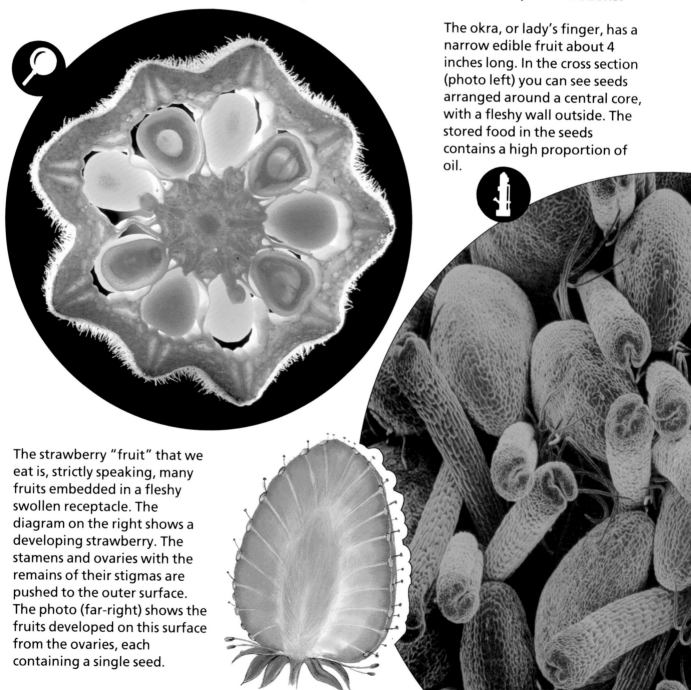

The strawberry "fruit" that we eat is, strictly speaking, many fruits embedded in a fleshy swollen receptacle. The diagram on the right shows a developing strawberry. The stamens and ovaries with the remains of their stigmas are pushed to the outer surface. The photo (far-right) shows the fruits developed on this surface from the ovaries, each containing a single seed.

The fruit of the dandelion is very characteristic. It consists of a single seed enclosed in the remains of the ovary. This has a stalk above which ends in a pappus – a whorl of feathery hairs. A fruiting head contains many of these fruits, making up the familiar dandelion "clock." The photo (right) shows ripe dandelion fruits. The pappus is a useful parachute, allowing the seed to travel with the wind and fall to earth slowly. With this help, the seeds can disperse far away from the parent.

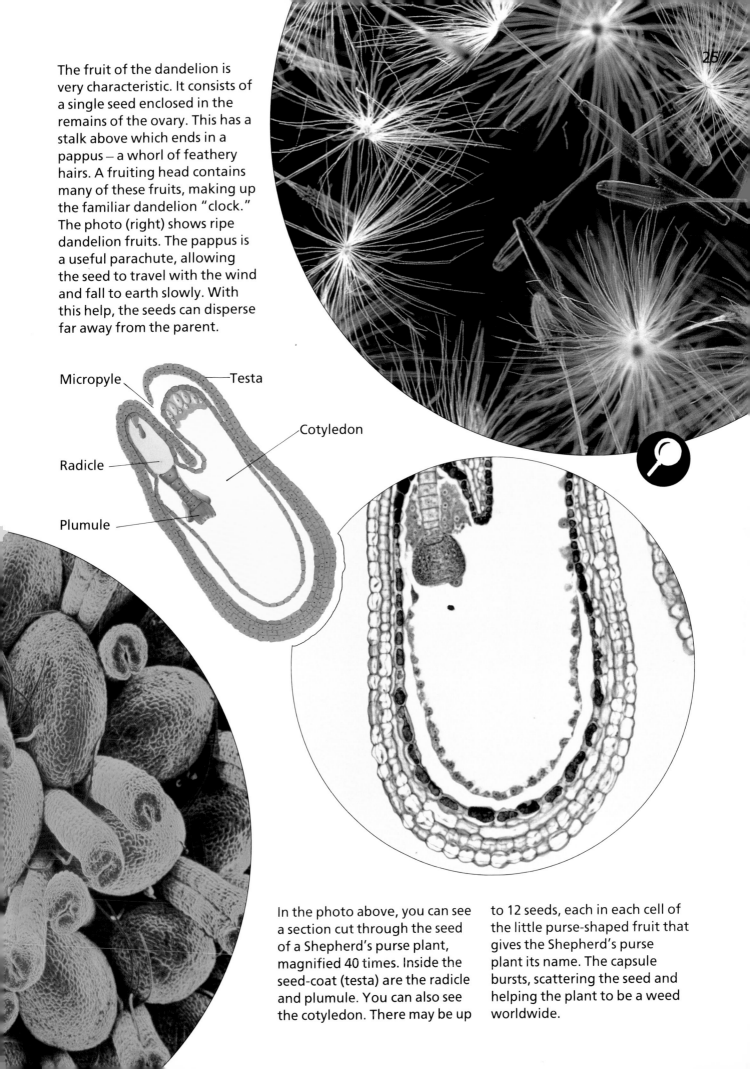

Micropyle

Testa

Cotyledon

Radicle

Plumule

In the photo above, you can see a section cut through the seed of a Shepherd's purse plant, magnified 40 times. Inside the seed-coat (testa) are the radicle and plumule. You can also see the cotyledon. There may be up to 12 seeds, each in each cell of the little purse-shaped fruit that gives the Shepherd's purse plant its name. The capsule bursts, scattering the seed and helping the plant to be a weed worldwide.

PESTS AND PARASITES

Just like us, plants suffer from diseases. These may be caused by bacteria, viruses or fungi. They are also eaten by many animals, especially insects. Some of these help to spread disease from plant to plant as they feed. For example, aphids spread many viral diseases, such as leaf-roll in potatoes, by sucking sap from one plant then another. Fungi attack many plants causing diseases such as mildew, rust, or "damping-off" of seedlings. Some fungi attack just one part of a plant. Others send threads through most of their host. Some flowering plants are parasites. Mistletoe, for example, grows into a host such as an apple tree and gets nourishment from it. Another parasite, dodder, is shown on this page.

The photo below shows an ear of wheat affected by a fungus called *Fusarium*, one of many fungi that can attack crop plants. Other kinds of Fusarium produce wilt disease in garden plants such as peas and beans. The fungus builds up in the soil if the same type of plant is grown each year.

Dodder is a reddish climbing plant of the bindweed family with no chlorophyll. It has a root when it first germinates but sends up a shoot that twines around a suitable plant. Once it has got a grip, suckers grow into the stem of the host. From then on, the dodder gets all its food through these special suckers, called haustoria, and its root shrivels away. Dodder has flowers, but its leaves are tiny scales. In the photo above, you can see a cross section of a nettle stem with dodder growing on it. The dodder looks pink. Its haustoria have penetrated the nettle.

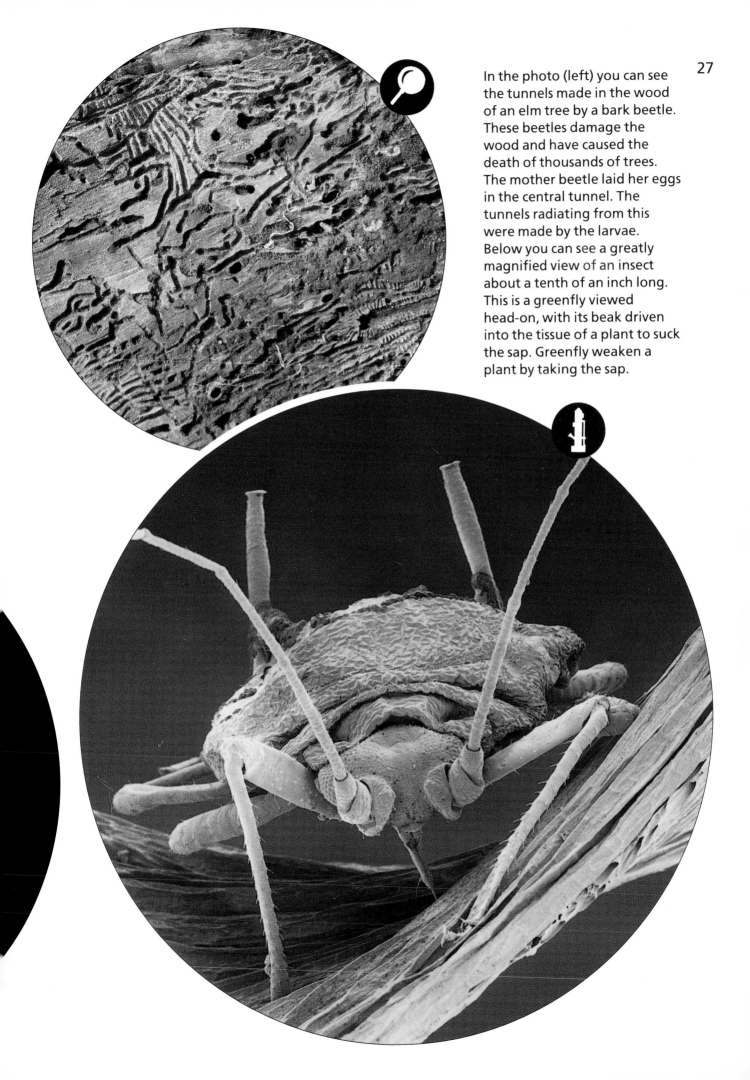

In the photo (left) you can see the tunnels made in the wood of an elm tree by a bark beetle. These beetles damage the wood and have caused the death of thousands of trees. The mother beetle laid her eggs in the central tunnel. The tunnels radiating from this were made by the larvae. Below you can see a greatly magnified view of an insect about a tenth of an inch long. This is a greenfly viewed head-on, with its beak driven into the tissue of a plant to suck the sap. Greenfly weaken a plant by taking the sap.

PRACTICAL PROJECTS

You can discover a great deal about nature's miniature world with just a hand lens. But to see greater detail you will need a home microscope like that shown on page 4. The objects you wish to study must be mounted on a glass slide. They must be made so that light can shine through them, so you may need to cut very thin slices of plant. To pick out the different types of cell, and the structures within them, you will need special dyes to stain your specimen. The way to do this is outlined below. If you are going to try something tricky, it is worth getting help from an adult. You may be able to start your studies with some ready-made slides bought from a microscope supplier.

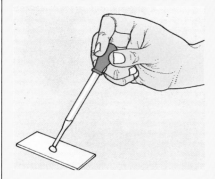

To prepare a slide of cells, place a drop of clean water containing them on the glass.

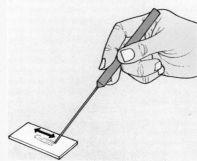

With a wire loop that has been sterilized in a flame, spread the fluid thinly.

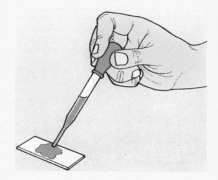

Add a small drop of staining dye to the cells and leave for a few minutes.

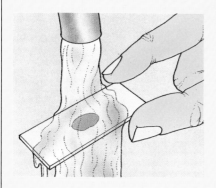

Wash off the dye with water or alcohol. You can stain with another, contrasting dye.

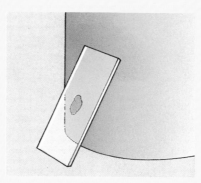

Leave the slide to dry. You can speed up drying by warming the slide over a flame.

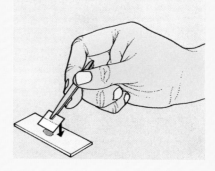

Place the cover slip (a thin square of glass) over the stained cells.

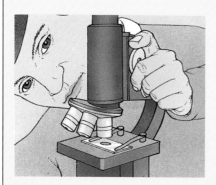

Put the slide on the microscope stage and position the mirror to give you good illumination.

Select the objective lens you want, then move the eyepiece up or down to focus.

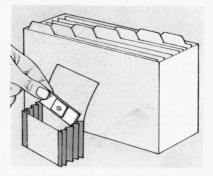

Keep your prepared slides in a cardboard wallet made by folding a thin sheet of card.

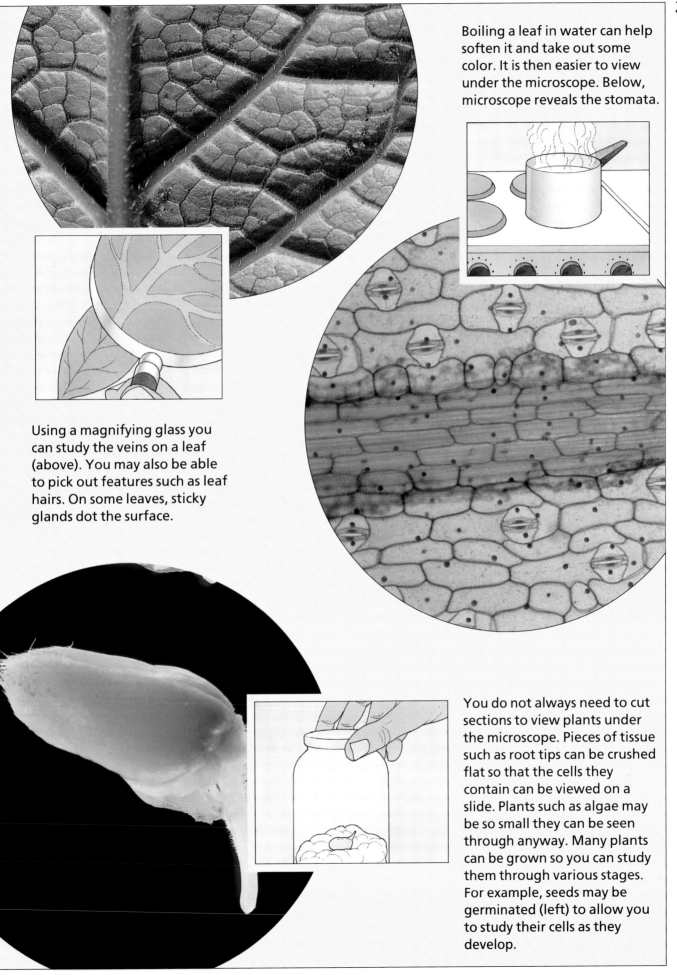

Boiling a leaf in water can help soften it and take out some color. It is then easier to view under the microscope. Below, microscope reveals the stomata.

Using a magnifying glass you can study the veins on a leaf (above). You may also be able to pick out features such as leaf hairs. On some leaves, sticky glands dot the surface.

You do not always need to cut sections to view plants under the microscope. Pieces of tissue such as root tips can be crushed flat so that the cells they contain can be viewed on a slide. Plants such as algae may be so small they can be seen through anyway. Many plants can be grown so you can study them through various stages. For example, seeds may be germinated (left) to allow you to study their cells as they develop.

MICROPHOTOGRAPHY

Some of the photographs in this book were taken using a camera with special close-up lenses that magnify the subject in much the same way as a hand-lens would magnify them for your eye. Others, with greater magnification, like the stem section on page 18, were taken by fitting a camera to the eyepiece of a scientific microscope. Such photos are known as photomicrographs. The colors in these are often those of stains used, rather than natural colors. If you have a home microscope you can take your own photomicrographs. You will need a single lens reflex camera and a special camera attachment. Many images in this book were produced using scanning electron microscopes.

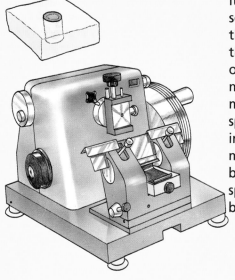

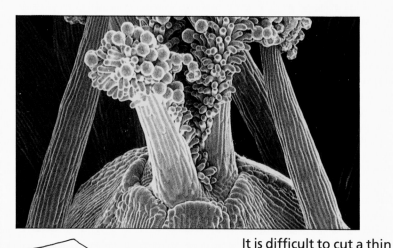

It is difficult to cut a thin section by hand. So very thin sections, like that of the stem above, are often made using a machine called a microtome. The specimen is embedded in a wax block. The microtome cuts the block and the enclosed specimen like a fine bacon slicer.

There are two main types of electron microscope. In a transmission type, a beam of electrons is passed through an extremely thin slice of tissue and an image is produced on a viewing screen. On a scanning electron microscope (an SEM), a fine beam of electrons is moved across the surface of the tissue for reflections to be collected and used to create an image on a television type of screen. Using an SEM, realistic 3-D images are produced. But as with all types of microscope specimens, the tissues and organs are no longer alive. The slide preparation process kills live cells. The colors on photos produced using an SEM are false colors added in processing.

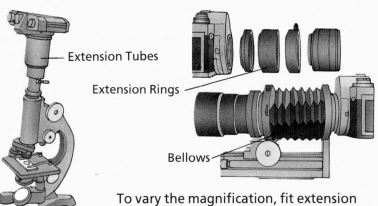

Extension Tubes

Extension Rings

Bellows

To vary the magnification, fit extension rings or bellows to the camera attachment.

GLOSSARY

axillary in the angle above where a leaf joins a stem.

bacteria small organisms without chlorophyll but with a cell wall and a simple nucleus that reproduce quickly by splitting. Some cause diseases, others are useful.

capsule a structure with a tough wall, such as that containing the spores of mosses.

cell one of the building blocks of which living things are made. Plants consist of many cells. Some may be specialized for particular jobs.

chitin a tough substance related to sugar that makes up the cell wall of fungi.

frond the large divided leaf of a fern, or the flattened body of a seaweed.

gemmae a special clump of cells developed for asexual reproduction in plants.

gills in fungi such as mushrooms, one of the vertical sheets of tissue under the cap that bear the spores.

haustoria an outgrowth from a parasite that penetrates the body of its host and extracts food.

hyphae the branching filaments that make up the body of many fungi.

magnification the number of times larger that an object seen through a lens or microscope appears compared with its true size.

microtome an instrument for cutting sections for light microscopy.

nodule a small lump, such as that housing bacteria in the roots of peas.

ovule the "egg" of a seed plant that after fertilization develops into the seed.

parasite an organism that lives on or in another one, taking nourishment from it and doing no good in return.

pigment a substance that is colored. The green of plants is caused by a pigment, chlorophyll. Other plant pigments include yellows, reds and purples.

prothallus the small fern plant that develops from a spore, then reproduces sexually to give the large familiar fronded fern.

sorus an area under a fern frond where the sporangia are clustered.

sporangium a hollow capsule in which spores are produced.

spore a resting or dispersal stage of a plant, usually single-celled, produced without sexual reproduction.

sporophyte a stage in the life history of a plant that produces spores, rather than undergoing sexual reproduction.

thallus the body of a simple plant such as a liverwort. Usually small, and not divided into stem, leaves and roots.

tracheid a cell that has elongated and developed thick, pitted walls and lost its cell contents. Its function is to conduct water through the plant.

WEIGHTS AND MEASURES

mm = millimeter 10mm = 1cm = 4/10 inch
cm = centimeter 100cm = 1m = 3 1/3 feet
m = meter 1,000m = 1km = 6/10 mile
km = kilometer
lb = pound g = gram 1,000g = 1kg = 2lb 3 ounces
kg = kilogram

0.1 = 1/10
0.01 = 1/100
0.001 = 1/1,000

INDEX

Photographic Credits:
Cover and pages 6, 8l, 9t, 13t, 14, 15 both, 16b, 17 both, 21t and m, 22l, 23 both, 24 both, 25t and 29m and b: Science Photo Library; pages 7 both, 8r, 9b, 10, 10-11, 11 all, 12, 13b, 16l, 18, 19 both, 21b, 22r, 25b, 26 both, 27 both, 29t and 30: Biophoto Associates.